"WE'RE SORRY!
YOUR FRIENDS, THE GOOD GUYS."

MEET MR. WOLF

THE BIG BAAAAD WOLF!

Hey you, get over here! Don't be scared . . . come a little bit closer.

Oh, I know what it is. You're afraid because . . . I'm the big bad wolf, right? I'm not surprised. I've heard it all! I'm the villain in every story. And sure, I've done bad things before, but it's easy to judge a book by its cover.

The name's Wolf. And if you're here, it's because you've heard things about me and my crew: the Good Guys (*formerly* the Bad Guys—trust me!).

The word on the street is that we're bad to the bone, known for epic heists, great disguises, and legendary chases. Some say that we're *always* up to no good, but don't believe everything you hear. We've changed! After a lifetime of crime, the Bad Guys faced our biggest job yet: going good. Easy, right? Wrong!

So, you think you're ready to join the crew and become a Good Guy yourself? I dig it! Let's give you the lowdown.

DreamWorks

the BAD GUYS 2

MOVIE GUIDE

THE GOOD, THE BAD, AND EVERYTHING IN BETWEEN

By Shelby Curran

Scholastic Inc.

Book design by Sophia La Torre and Stacie Zucker

ISBN 978-93-5954-653-7
Printed in India at Acme Print O Pac. Pvt. Ltd. Noida.

First printing 2025

This reptint edition: August 2025

TABLE OF CONTENTS

MEET THE ~~BAD~~ GOOD GUYS

WOLF

"I THOUGHT IT WAS **OBVIOUS . . .** WE'RE GOING TO GO **GOOD!**"

—*Mr. Wolf*

NAME: Wolf

ALIAS: The Big Bad Wolf, sometimes disguised as Mr. Poodleton or Mr. Buck Wolfford

CRIMINAL ACTIVITY:

- Carjacked a one-of-a-kind set of wheels
- Masterminded epic bank robberies
- Stole the Golden Dolphin from the Gala for Goodness
- Snatched Mr. Moon's watch at the altar
- Led the Bad Guys . . . to go good?

TOP SECRET

MEET MR. SNAKE

THE SNEAKY SERPENTINE!

Say hello to Snake! He's a serpentine safe-cracking machine. Imagine Houdini with no arms. Pretty cool, right?

Snake is a guy who says the glass is half empty and then steals it from you. He is skilled at sliding into hidden spaces and places—undetected!

It's easy to think that a sneaky snake couldn't slither into anyone's hearts, but take it from me: Snake is the best bud you could ask for. His dry *scaly* humor may make him grumpy most of the time, but no heist would be complete without him trying to take a *bite* out of our enemies!

SNAKE

"I MADE A LOT OF **ENEMIES** IN MY TIME . . . I MEAN, **A *LOT*!"**

—*Mr. Snake*

NAME: Snake

ALIAS: Mr. Grumpy Pants

CRIMINAL ACTIVITY:

- Broke into Mr. Ho's Pet Store
- Ate all the mice at Mr. Ho's Pet Store
- Ate all the canaries at Mr. Ho's Pet Store
- Ate all the guinea pigs at Mr. Ho's Pet Store . . . you get the point!

TOP SECRET

MEET MS. TARANTULA

THE WEBS MASTER!

Ready for who's up next? You've been hacked!

Tarantula is a key part of this cool crew. She's our hacking superstar, pocket search engine, and traveling tech wizard. We call her Webs, and it's easy to see why. Eight legs? More like eight gazillion ways to hack the Internet! Talk about beast mode!

Back in the day, she proved herself worthy of joining our gang during an epic heist in Cairo. After outwitting our enemies during a heart-racing chase, I knew she was the perfect missing piece of our team: our own in-house Geek Squad!

TARANTULA

"LIGHTS OUT, EVERYONE ON COMMS, DO YOU COPY?"

—*Ms. Tarantula*

NAME: Tarantula

ALIAS: Webs

CRIMINAL ACTIVITY:

- Hacked the police dispatch
- Hijacked the traffic light control system
- Infiltrated a crane's manual override
- Shut down security cameras
- You name it—it doesn't have a firewall anymore!

TOP SECRET

MEET MR. SHARK

THE FIN-TASTIC MASTER OF DISGUISE!

Daa da. Daa da. Dun, dun, dun . . . Shark attack!

Mr. Shark is the master of disguise and apex predator of a thousand faces. Shark's greatest trick? Stealing the *Mona Lisa*—disguised as Mona Lisa.

Not only can he dress any part, but he also possesses Oscar-worthy acting skills. Italian wedding planner? He's on it! Unsuspecting lady attending a charity gala? No problemo. Wacky security guard in a billionaire's mansion? Easy peasy.

No fins about it, Shark can fool anyone with a fashion facade. His costumes and disguises work like a charm, every heist! Dig that!

SHARK

"KEEP IT COOL, **BABY!"**

—*Mr. Shark*

NAME: Shark

ALIAS: Big Tuna

CRIMINAL ACTIVITY:

- Disguised as a construction worker
- Disguised as a scientist's dad visiting the lab—ready for a catch!
- Disguised as a rich woman
- Disguised as Marco the wedding planner
- Disguised as a security guard for a powerful billionaire
- Fooled literally anybody—and will do so again!

TOP SECRET

MEET MR. PIRANHA

THE MUSCLE MANIAC!

What's up, *papito*? Rounding out the crew is Piranha: a loose cannon with a short fuse willing to scrap with anyone or anything. I mean, have you seen the muscles on this guy?! Not to mention those chompers. He's a mean, lean fighting machine.

Piranha is brave, fearless, crazy, and everything in between. Get him riled up, and his muscles (and razor-sharp teeth) are sure to teach any enemy a real lesson.

Another superpower? His awesome ability to release hazardous, stinky gas when a heist gets stressful. He'll have his enemies holding their breath, alright.

PIRANHA

“CRAZY IS WHAT I BRING TO THE PARTY, CHICO!”

—Mr. Piranha

NAME: Piranha

ALIAS: The Muscle

CRIMINAL ACTIVITY:

- Fought his foes with mighty muscles
- Shredded his enemies with his razor-sharp teeth
- Released smelly, noxious emissions—beware!
- Blew a fuse by . . . blowing HIS fuse!

TOP SECRET

BREAKING NEWS

THE WORLD'S ~~SMOOTHEST AND SLICKEST CRIMINALS~~ UNLIKELY HEROES!

And that's the crew! They're born eccentrics—it's true! But when you're born us, you don't win many popularity contests. We may be misfits who are different in our own ways, but you know, I'd say we're the same in many ways, too.

See, it would've been easier to stay bad forever. After all, we were ***so*** good at it! These are the cards we've been dealt, and we ***could've*** continued to play 'em. It's not easy to change after a long history of being the world's biggest and baddest criminals. Especially when people still see us as monsters—no matter what we do.

So, how did the ***Bad*** Guys become the ***Good*** Guys? It's time to catch our newest member up to speed.

"EVERYONE SAY 'ROBBERY'!"
—Mr. Wolf

SETTING THE (CRIME) SCENE

In the good ol' days, the best buds and I were at the height of cementing our legacy as the coolest and smoothest criminals of all time. Rob the national bank and steal all the cash? Done. Break into the Louvre and snatch the oldest and most famous art pieces? Finito.

But I started to wonder what it'd be like if the world *loved* us instead of being scared of us.

It started with a feeling deep inside—an instinct I've never felt before. *Something* compelled me to save an old lady from falling down a flight of stairs—after a purse snatch gone wrong—and I felt "the wag" of goodness for the first time. You know, that warm fuzzy feeling of being appreciated and applauded.

But getting distracted during our mission to steal the Golden Dolphin was *not* an option. I had to resist!

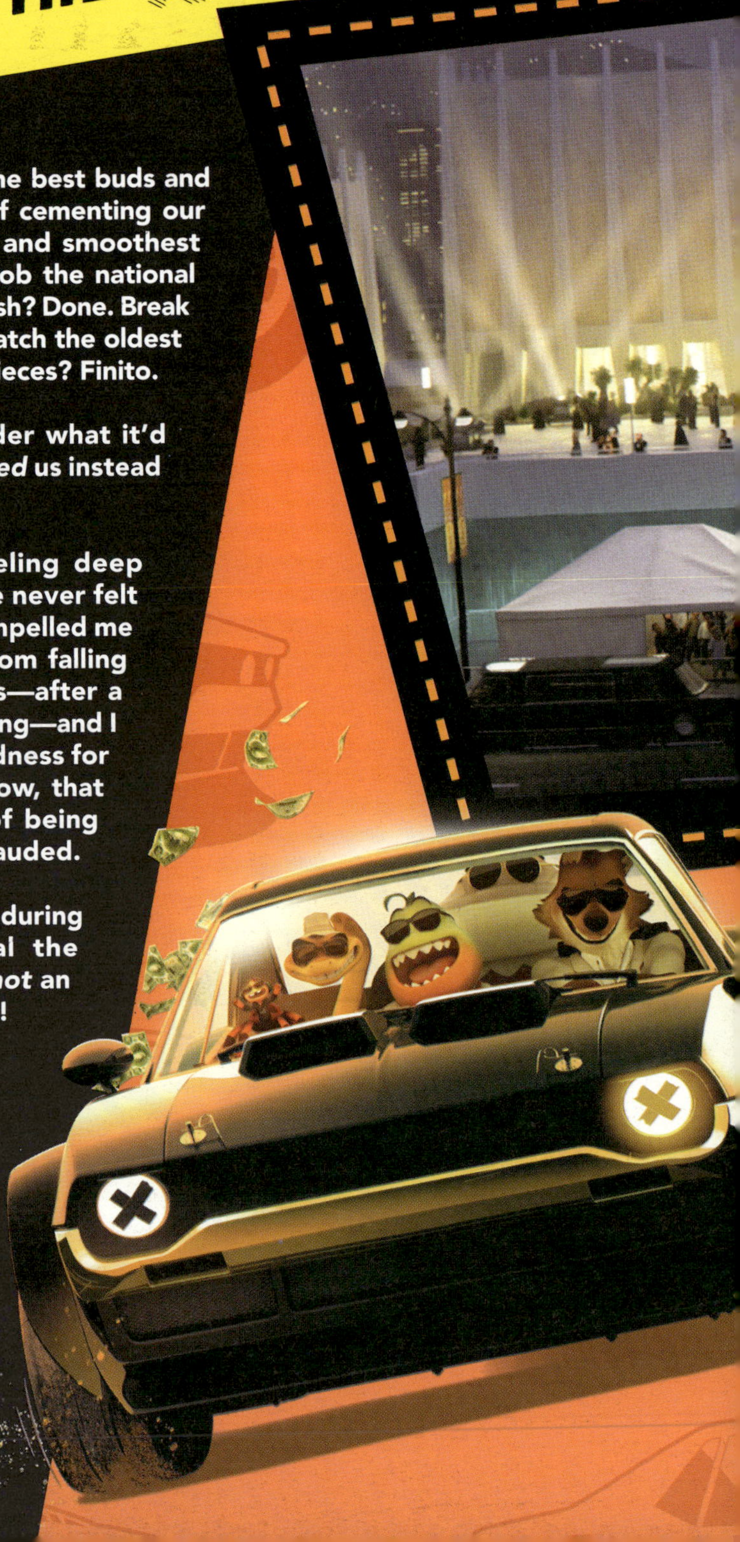

To escape being arrested, we made a deal to go good—you know, *only* to avoid jail time.

After the wag, nothing ever felt the same. It was hard to ignore that *gooood* feeling.

In the end, we realized that we can still tap into all the things that make us, well, us—all while doing just a *little* good along the way. But even though we believed it, the world didn't. We were framed (by an evil guinea pig, if you can believe it), sent to prison, and tested with our greatest mission yet: clearing our names.

Now here we are: the newly minted Good Guys! It's time for a fresh start, and we're ready to use our tricks and talents for good. What could go wrong?

Since you're the newest member of the Good Guys, we're going to show you the ropes. Let's make like a wolf and get the pack out of here!

FRIENDS OR FOES?

Over our time as seasoned criminals (and recently, heroes), we've been a lot of places and seen a lot of faces. We've been fought, framed, and downright foiled, but we've always come out the other side as a team.

As a Good Guy yourself, you're going to need to know who to trust and who to watch out for. After all, the world is still filled with crime, robberies, and maybe even copycat criminals, and it won't be easy to keep our names clear. We've gotta fit in with the rest of the world, make new names for ourselves, and stay out of trouble.

So, there should be no surprises, right? Nah. Nothing is ever as it seems. Always be on the lookout for a twist and always expect the unexpected. Capiche?

GOVERNOR DIANE FOXINGTON

Meet Diane Foxington: our elected governor. She's all about helping the community, making improvements to the state, and blah, blah, blah, a bunch of other boring stuff.

Sure, she might have a pretty face (don't tell the other guys I said that), but there's so much more to Diane than meets the eye. She's sneaky, sharp, and smart. Hey, you know what they say—a wolf and a fox aren't so different after all, right?

"I'M STILL ME; I'M JUST ME ON THE RIGHT SIDE!"
—The Crimson Paw

THE CRIMSON PAW

THE CRIMSON PAW

The Crimson Paw is a legendary bandit! She's the queen of cons. Can you believe she stole the Zumpango Diamond twice? Once for profit and the second time just for fun! I mean, who does that?!

Never identified, never caught, the Crimson Paw goes down in history as one of the greatest criminals of all time. Or at least she used to be. This former criminal mastermind *also* went good. After accomplishing every mission in her wildest and baddest dreams, the Crimson Paw wondered where to go from there—and felt the wag, too.

And who would've thought she'd be the governor in disguise? The world thinks *someone else* is responsible for being the Crimson Paw (and fooling the world from right under our whiskers), but Diane's secret is safe with us.

Or at least it was, until a copycat crew tricked us into helping them commit a crime and threatened to upload a video revealing the governor's true identity to the world! Yeah, things got weird. I told you nothing is ever as it seems.

PROFESSOR RUPERT MARMALADE IV

Professor Marmalade *had* the perfect image. As a recipient of the Good Samaritan Award, that little dude had the entire city at his fingertips. Whispers on the street said he was second to Mother Teresa. Give me a break!

The crew learned the hard way that this tricky guinea pig has a bad side (don't we all?), and his best behavior was all an act! First, Marmalade claimed that he could teach us to be good and show the world we *had* changed. But at the Gala for Goodness, he framed and blamed us for stealing the meteorite on display. What a betrayal!

It was all part of an epic evil plan to use the meteorite as an ultimate power source! Marmalade harnessed it to control an army of guinea pigs and steal his *own* charity funds throughout the city. To stop him, Snake faked his defection and carried out a legendary switcheroo—swapping the real meteorite with a fake one. Take that! Marmalade was exposed as the true thief and framed as the Crimson Paw.

Just when we thought we'd seen the last of Marmalade (finally proving we *are* good guys), he began plotting something *big* from prison. Marmalade was not happy about being blamed for the Crimson Paw's crimes—not one bit. When a new crew of criminals asked him to help pull off the greatest gold heist in history, Marmalade saw an opportunity for sweet revenge. As a MacGuffinite expert, he knew exactly what they should do.

"WE CAN ALL AGREE THERE IS A FLOWER OF **GOODNESS** INSIDE **ALL OF US**, WAITING TO **BLOSSOM!**"

—Professor Marmalade

"ADMIT IT, **YOU MISSED ME!**"

—Professor Marmalade

POLICE CHIEF

(REAL NAME IS MISTY LUGGINS)

That's Chief (who was recently promoted to commissioner—what a big shot!) and she's in charge of the police department.

So what if she's made it her entire life's mission to catch us in the act. In the good ol' days, we got a kick out of running Chief and her crew around the whole city. But now Chief is our partner in crime! I mean, our partner in *justice*. (Sorry, pal, it's just an expression.)

She took a leap of faith and trusted us when we needed it most. When a copycat bandit emerged from the shadows, Chief was struggling to get to the bottom of the mystery. Lucky for her, I know *exactly* how a criminal thinks. She needed to solve a big case, and the Good Guys needed to prove to the world that we've changed for good this time. You know, a mutual back-scratching kinda thing.

Somewhere in that big booming heart of hers, Chief believed in us! Thanks to our teamwork, we closed the case, found the MacGuffinite connection between all the stolen artifacts, and identified hot leads. Niiiice!

MISTY LUGGINS
Expires: 10/19/2021
URITY

TIFFANY FLUFFIT

LIVE TV

Live from the scene of the crime, it's Tiffany Fluffit! Channel 6, Action News!

She's always reporting on our antics and telling the citizens what they need to know. Erhm, she doesn't always get the story straight—maybe it's all "fluff!"—but hey, no press is bad press, am I right?

Tonight's headline? *The Nefarious Fivesome Leaves Crime Behind!* Any comment?

8:24PM
74°
"AND I, TIFFANY FLUFFIT, AM FIRST ON THE SCENE!" —Tiffany Fluffit

VOTE MAUREEN

Every great undercover governor needs a campaign aide for reelection, right?

Maureen always makes sure that Diane gets to press conferences on time and answers to all the responsibilities that come with leading the state—and hey, that ain't easy when a fox is leading a double life. That's for sure! After all, Maureen doesn't understand why a do-good governor would *ever* be friends with an ex-con like me.

CRAIG

Cha-ching!

Say hello to Craig, the branch manager at Complete Trust Bank, a place that obviously has a lot of *trust* in me and the guys.

Alright, so I may have applied for a job at the bank after robbing it three times. But how am I supposed to prove that I've changed if no one will give me a chance? *Come on,* Craig!

MR. JEREMIAH MOON

LIVE TV

Mr. Moon is a big-shot space tycoon and proud owner of MOON-X Space Tours. His next great idea? Installing a high-tech space battery that will supply Earth with free Wi-Fi—all the way from space! So what. Big deal.

As if his business ventures weren't enough, Mr. Moon is getting hitched! Invitation only, of course—unless you crash the wedding to steal his custom watch and gain control of the MOON-X Rocket site, all because you're being forced to, erhm, I mean, celebrate the happy couple on their big day. Nothing to see here!

HANDSOME JORGE GARCIA

It's a RUUUMBLE! This tough guy? He's the current reigning world champion of the Lords of Lucha Tournament. The only thing he loves more than winning tournaments? Himself—and the way he looks!

When he was up against a shifty new competitor, the ol' crew stepped in during the fight to defend the Belt of Guatelamango. But when the plan didn't go according to plan, we removed his opponent's mask and got mobbed by, well, the mob. Epic!

SUSAN/DOOM

DOOM

As if the idea of Mr. Grumpy Pants himself having a girlfriend wasn't hard enough to believe . . . he accidentally fell in love with an undercover criminal, too?! Talk about a match made in heaven! It would take a real sugar beak of a woman to cheer up Snake. He doesn't even like birthdays, much less romance. *Gross!*

The gang was first introduced to this lady crow as Susan, who was squawking sweet nothings to our buddy Snake. After meeting on a city bus, these two knew they were made for each other. Sure, maybe Snake slithered into her heart, or maybe it was all an epic setup! Watch out, Casanova!

Things changed *very* fast! Under the alias Susan, she went from bamboozling Snake to conning the crew. We thought she was stealing a hot-dog-shaped-food-truck-turned-getaway-car to help us escape the chaos at the Lords of Lucha Tournament! But really, Susan had big plans to knock us out with breath mints and kidnap us. Who woulda thought?!

Her *real* name's Doom—a copycat criminal who joined her own crew of "Bad Girls," studied our tricks, and roped us into a heist—against our will. Hey, we should take it as a compliment, right?

"SHE **OUT-SNAKED** A SNAKE! IF THAT'S NOT **TRUE LOVE**, I DON'T KNOW WHAT IS!"
—Mr. Snake

"YOU MAY NOW CALL ME **DOOM!**"
—a.k.a. Susan

"**SNAKEY WAKEY** DON'T LIKE TO SHARE, DO HE? UNLESS IT'S **KISSES!**"
—Susan

KITTY KAT

KITTY KAT

Peekaboo! Meet Kitty Kat, the criminal mastermind and leader of the Bad Girls copy*cat* crew. Don't be fooled by her sweet feline face. Behind her green eyes and bright smile is the bigger *badder* version of . . . me? Take it from someone with a decorated criminal résumé—I would know!

Kitty Kat and her gang of associates set out to pull off the biggest heist the world has *ever* seen.

STEP 1: Kidnap the *former* Bad Guys and force them into helping the Bad Girls (the purest form of flattery!).

STEP 2: Team up to steal Mr. Moon's watch.

STEP 3: Use the watch to break into the MOON-X launch site and control everything.

STEP 4: Initiate the MOON-X Rocket launch three days early.

STEP 5: Activate the MacGuffinite gold magnet from space and steal all the gold on Earth! *Cha-ching!*

What could go wrong? Nothing, of course, if the Good Guys didn't have their own plan brewing.

"PEEKABOO! THE NAME'S KITTY."
—Kitty Kat

PIGTAIL

PIGTAIL

Completing the copycat crew is Pigtail, also known as Buttersnout (at least according to Webs).

She's the smart, sharp engineer of the Bad Girls. And as a huge crime nerd, Pigtail is a superfan of the Bad Guys. I dig it!

The gang first laid eyes on this sneaky swine at the Lords of Lucha Tournament. Disguised as a star luchadora, Pigtail battled the legendary Handsome Jorge Garcia in the ring. Her mission? Create the perfect setup for the former Bad Guys and bring them to Kitty Kat while securing the MacGuffinite-made Belt of Guatelamango! But when the guys jumped into the ring and exposed the mystery pig by removing her mask, madness ensued! The crowd was *squealing* in chaos!

It's true that Pigtail and the guys got off to a rocky start—you know, between the battle-ring showdown, the kidnapping, and of course we can't forget the tricking-us-into-being-a-part-of-a-heist thing. But you know what? Pigtail became a true friend in the end.

“IT WAS THE PLEASURE OF A LIFETIME TO KICK THE BUTTS OF MY HEROES.”
—Pigtail

MR. SOLIMAN

Talk about a bad billionaire! Back during Webs's first heist ever, we took down THE billionaire of the century and stole a sweet ride! He's got nothing on us—and money talks! It was legendary.

But Mr. Soliman never forgets a face (especially his, which he could stare at all day, preferably when it's on the front of *Billionaire's Digest Magazine*). He almost blew the guys' cover at Mr. Moon's wedding. We crashed the party in order to steal Mr. Moon's watch, forced into helping Kitty Kat and her crew. But when Mr. Soliman interrupted the ceremony in an outburst—ruining our plan and claiming that *I* was disguised as the bride—we had to improvise.

Mr. Soliman created the perfect distraction for the gang to execute our new and improved plan! I pretended to faint into Mr. Moon's arms, swapping his MOON-X watch for a fake one. Step one: complete! Then Pigtail blinded Mr. Soliman with the spotlights so he couldn't see the switcheroo. At the perfect moment, Shark, who was disguised as the officiant, snuck away from the altar so that Kitty Kat could put the real bride in my place. And for the last step? Doom soared over the altar with Snake, who completed the perfect wedding dress quick change, and flew me away undetected. No one suspected a thing!

“YOU **BAD GUYS** ARE **THE WORST!**”

—*Mr. Soliman*

BAD GUYS

It takes a Bad Guy to catch a Bad Guy... or should I say, a Bad Girl? Anyway, we're the originals. The real deals! Safe crackers, master hackers, con men of the highest order.

VS. BAD GIRLS

Though, I have to admit, these notorious copy cats are pretty good at fighting. And plotting an out of this world heist. And tricking most of the city. And... alright they are pretty good at what they do.

LOCATION DETECTED

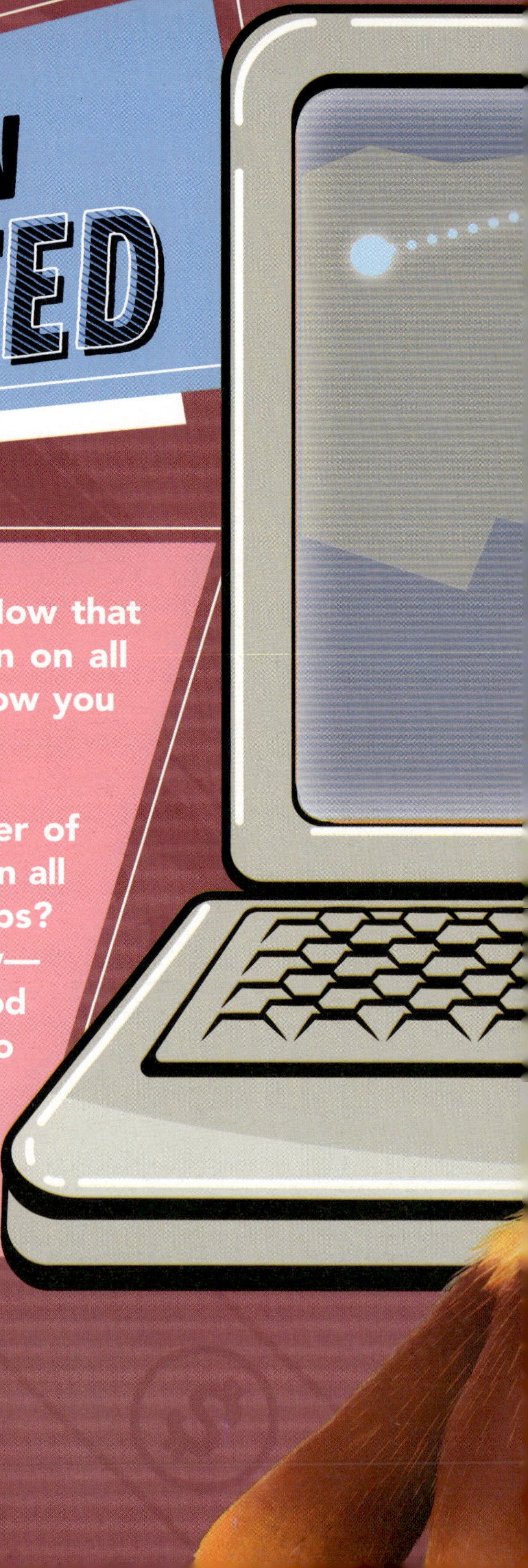

Still with me, partner? Now that you've got the lowdown on all the *faces*, it's time to show you around all the *places*.

And what better member of the crew to clue you in on all the hot spots than Webs? She's got eyes on the city—at all times. The newly good Bad Guys always need to watch out for any evil plans or framing attempts brewing! Do you copy?

WEBS'S CONTROL ROOM

WPPST system override! Welcome to Webs's Control Room. It can be set up anywhere!

At the scene of any great heist, Webs has her comms systems ready to infiltrate any tech. She's a big part of making any mission a great success! Not only can she override any security system, but she can also track anywhere and anything in this city. Want to try it? Let's visit some hot spots—undetected.

OVERRIDE COMPLETE!

OLD BAD GUYS' LAIR

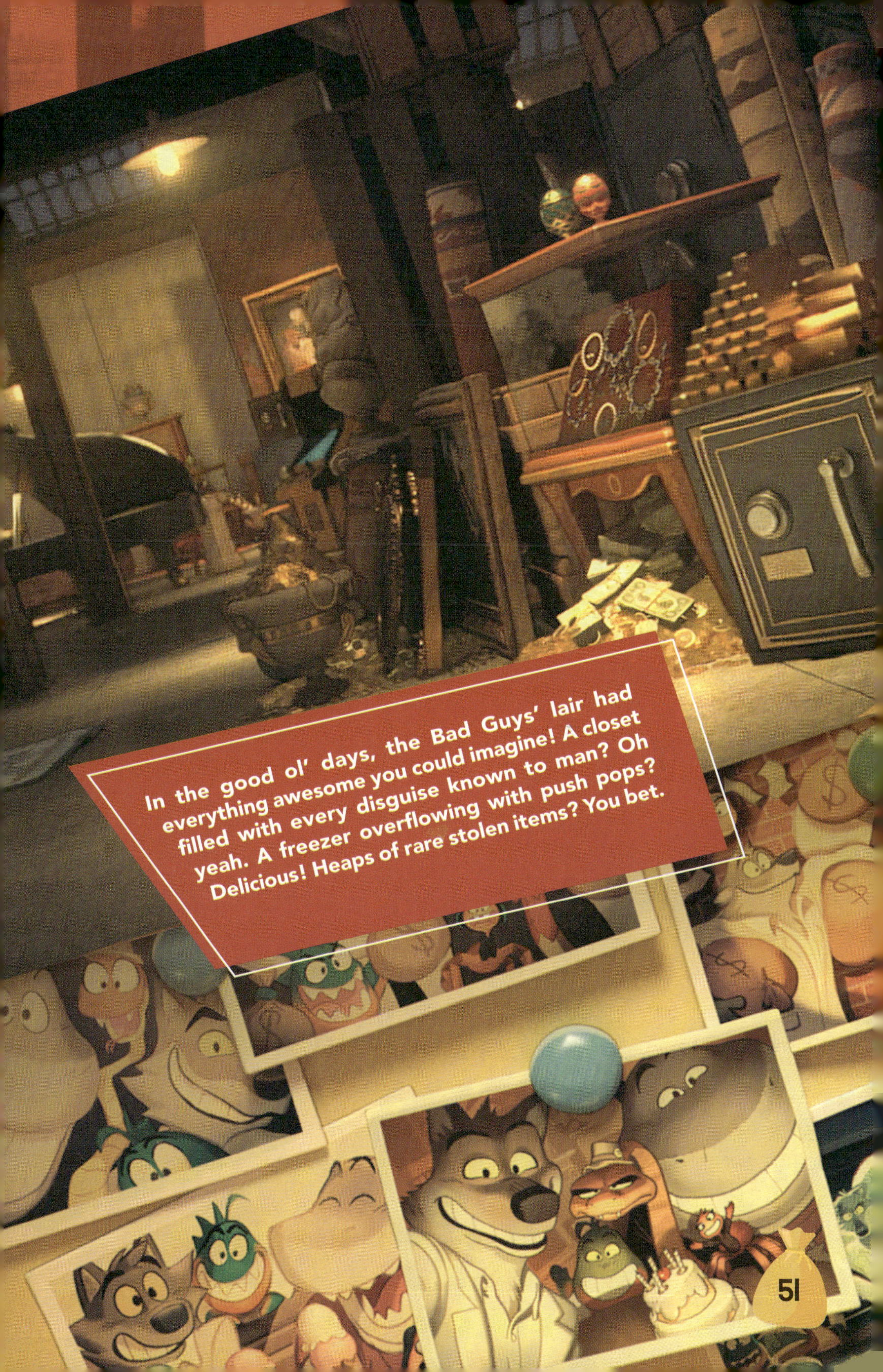

In the good ol' days, the Bad Guys' lair had everything awesome you could imagine! A closet filled with every disguise known to man? Oh yeah. A freezer overflowing with push pops? Delicious! Heaps of rare stolen items? You bet.

Now that we're the Good Guys, things *may* look a little different around here. The lair is overflowing with long overdue bills, a TV that barely works, and cheap folding chairs instead of furniture. But one thing hasn't changed: though it may not look like the coolest HQ, this is where I've made a home with my best pals.

NEW BAD GUYS' LAIR

THE DINER

Can you smell that cheap cup of joe? Mouthwatering!

The diner is the perfect place to sit back, relax, and read *The City Times* over breakfast.

Snake and I have many fond memories here. Like on his birthday, when the entire restaurant cowered at the sight of us in the room. That was back when the world had a reason to fear us!

But hey, on the bright side, a great way to not have to wait for coffee. I'm kidding!

THE COMPLETE TRUST BANK

Alright, alright, what can I say? We've had the best times here!

The Complete Trust Bank used to be a hot spot for our heists: stealing money, wreaking havoc, and being chased by cops in our getaway car.

But now the only action happening here is filling out job applications. Do you think knowing the ins and outs of how to rob a bank (as a *former* criminal) counts as relevant job experience? I've gotta pay the bills somehow!

POLICE STATION

At the police station, you can find ~~Chief~~ Commissioner Misty Luggins working on big cases with her team.

I think it's safe to say that we've been suspects on her radar more often than not. But now it's almost like the Good Guys are members of the crime-solving unit ourselves! Relax, Chief, I'm only kidding!

“DID YOU TOUCH MY BOARD? MY BOARD? **MY BEAUTIFUL BOARD?!”**

—Misty Luggins,
Police ~~Chief~~ Commissioner

MUSEUM OF FINE ARTS

Every year at the Museum of Fine Arts, the city gathers for the Good Samaritan Award ceremony, where the Golden Dolphin is presented to the most charitable citizen.

One of our biggest and coolest heists back as the Bad Guys was plotting to steal the Golden Dolphin from under the city's whiskers! Professor Rupert Marmalade IV was being honored and presented with the award—and now you know how that went.

But remember the magic of "the wag" that I was telling you about? Well, it was here where I first felt it! You know, that good feeling like when you're scratched between your ears? There's nothing like it. You could say it's my Good Guy origin story.

"AS FOR THE SCULPTURE, I THINK IT'S ABOUT **PERSPECTIVE.** IF YOU LOOK CLOSELY ENOUGH, EVEN **TRASH** CAN BE **RECYCLED** INTO SOMETHING **BEAUTIFUL.**"

—Governor Foxington

"I GUESS SOME THINGS **AREN'T ALWAYS** AS THEY **APPEAR.**"

—Mr. Wolf, disguised as Mr. Poodleton

PROFESSOR MARMALADE'S HOUSE

"RODENT'S GOT TASTE, OKAY!"
—Mr. Shark

Back when the guys were only *pretending* to go good, we were whisked away to Professor Marmalade's house.

On the outside, the five of us were villains, predators, and complete menaces to society. And since everyone thought Marmalade was the most charitable citizen the city had ever seen—and boy, were they wrong—he was in charge of teaching us how to be good. His real mission? Frame us and commit evil crimes himself!

But you know, it wasn't the worst place to spend some time. Marmalade's place is *faaaancy*! Way better than being arrested.

Do you feel that? It's a tingle of goodness! Here in Professor Marmalade's State-of-the-Art Sharing Lab-*or*-a-tory—also known as the inside of Marmalade's house—even the baddest of the bad can go good.

Now remember: Sharing is caring, always help others, and most of all, never suspect that a good guinea pig has a hidden agenda. Got it?

SUNNYSIDE LABORATORIES

Have you ever heard of a heist for good? Let's take a trip down memory lane to Sunnyside Laboratories.

After spending time at Marmalade's learning how to be kind and help others, it was time to put our *good* skills to the test. You see, we were *still* going to use all the things that made us who we are. Only this time, instead of committing crime, we wanted to commit *justice*.

The mission? Break into Sunnyside Laboratories, where innocent guinea pigs were being held hostage in the name of science! If we could release them, then we would show the world that we really have changed *for good*. But could Snake control his appetite?

GALA FOR GOODNESS

"I, RUPERT MARMALADE THE FOURTH, WILL TURN THE BAD GUYS INTO . . . THE GOOD GUYS!"
—Professor Marmalade

#CharityEventoftheYear, according to Professor Marmalade! How suspicious.

We're gonna be good tonight! Or at least that's what we were supposed to do. For once, it felt great to have everyone not fear us for a change. The gala-goers went gaga for us Bad Guys, and maybe that was what we needed to finally commit to a real change.

HIDEOUT OF THE GREAT CRIMSON PAW

Identity verified. Welcome, Diane! So, this is the hideout of the great Crimson Paw? Pretty cool.

"IT'S GOOD TO BE HOME."
—*Diane Foxington/ The Crimson Paw*

WE NEED EYES ON THE CITY!

SUCM (SUPER ULTRA CRAZY MAX)

It's true that things get sticky in here. It's prison, after all. Fights between friends, epic showdowns, and menacing interrogations!

LOCATION CLASSIFIED

CAIRO, EGYPT

Cairo is a cooool city, full of awesome history. Pyramids, pharaohs, tombs? Nah, I was talking about Bad Guys' history.

Did you know this was the place Tarantula joined us for her first-ever heist? Dig that! Here, we secured our black muscle car and stole it from right under Mr. Soliman's nose. What a sweet ride. Now *that's* history.

Things have certainly changed since Cairo. Not everyone believes it, but the Bad Guys went good—I'm telling you!

LORDS OF LUCHA TOURNAMENT

Are you ready to RUUUUMBLE? At the annual Lords of Lucha Tournament, one mighty *luchador* is crowned the world champion! From bumpin' banda music to mouthwatering food trucks, this action-packed event is a fan favorite.

The guys came to catch the copycat bandit, who had big plans to steal the MacGuffinite-made Belt of Guatelamango! But after we interrupted the epic showdown between Handsome Jorge Garcia and the mystery fighter (who we later learned was Pigtail in disguise), the Lords of Lucha Tournament not only became home to world-class fights but also infamous chases!

Watch out for the angry mob—let's bounce!

SANTA BARBARA ESTATE

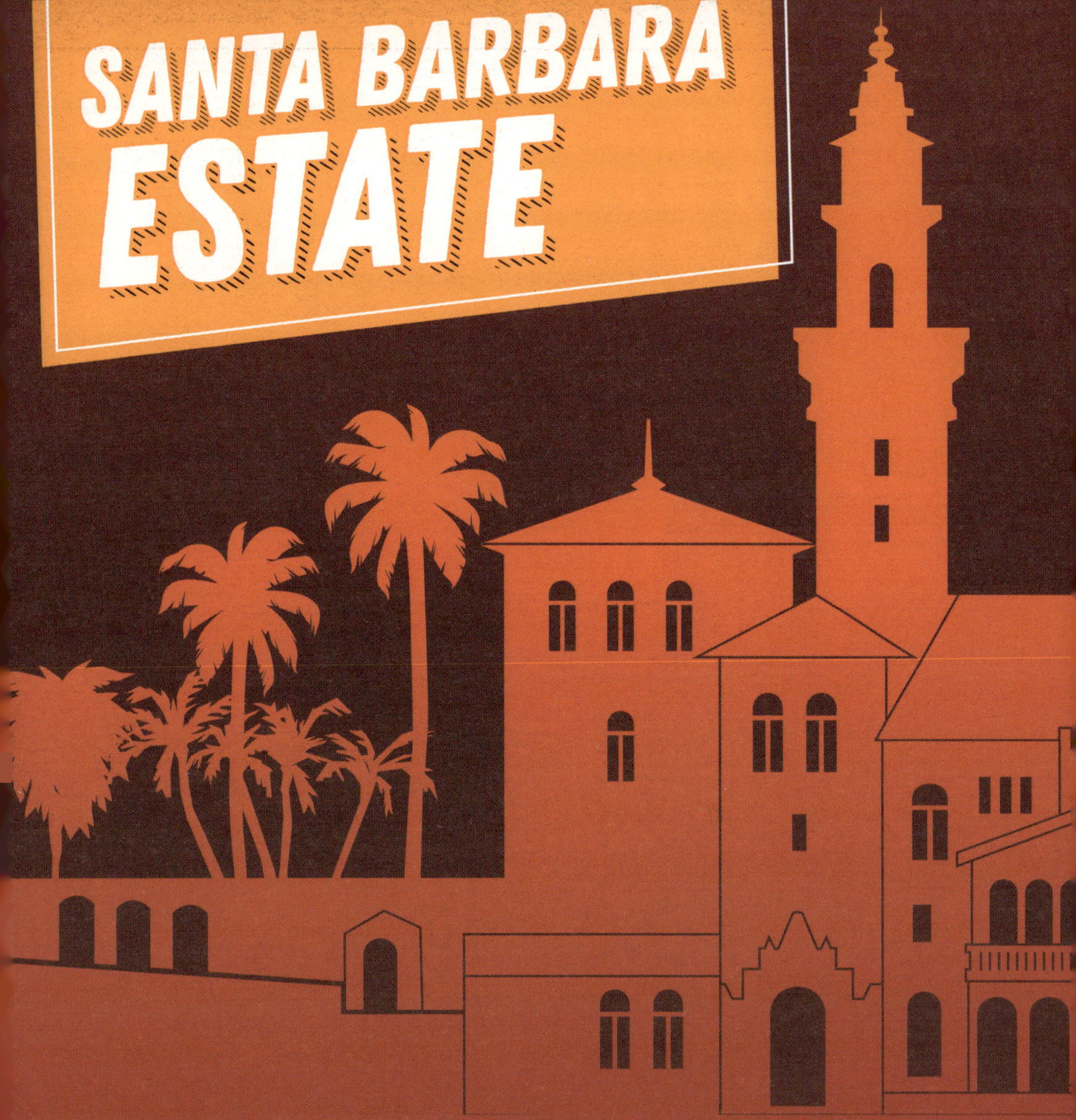

It doesn't get ritzier than Mr. Moon's Santa Barbara Estate!

With the estate grounds covered in glorious greens, majestic fountains, and tall palm trees—it's *heavenly*. Could you imagine owning a joint like this? An awesome mansion is the perfect place to throw a wedding, especially if the man of the hour is getting hitched.

WATCH OUT FOR WEDDING CRASHERS! BUT YOU DIDN'T HEAR THAT FROM ME.

MOON-X LAUNCH SITE

Ready for blastoff? Kitty Kat and her Bad Girls crew sure are. After the team successfully stole Mr. Moon's watch, the copycat crew had what they needed for the next phase of their evil mission. First, they handcuffed the guys to an abandoned hangar, and then they gave us a choice: either save ourselves or upload a video of Diane's true identity for the world to see. Ruthless!

These criminal masterminds broke into the MOON-X base after scanning fake visitor badges. After opening the gate to the launch site—undetected!—the girls suited up in astronaut gear and prepared for takeoff. But not so fast—the Crimson Paw showed up to *try* and save the day!

“THIS IS GETTING REAL!”

—Pigtail

YOU’RE UNDER ARREST… GOVERNOR’S ORDERS!

OUTER SPACE?!

MULTINATIONAL SPACE STATION

Time to learn your way around the MOON-X Rocket, pal. Are you ready for another heist for *good*?

After breaking free from the cuffs, the guys were faced with *everything* that was going wrong: Diane's true identity was revealed, the world was calling Marmalade a wrongfully accused criminal, and—maybe worst of all—the city turned their attention to *us* as the new criminals to blame. We had to clear our names, yet again, and save the world in the process.

Thanks to Chief's leap of faith and *awesome* police helicopter, we soared through the sky and broke into the rocket, right in the nick of time. The guys pulled off an action-packed mission, filled with twists, turns, zero-gravity weightlessness, and oh yeah, unlikely copycat-criminals-turned-friends?

Just as Snake and Piranha were about to float away to another galaxy with the MacGuffinite magnet stealing *all* the gold on Earth, we were saved! It's never too late to feel the wag of good.

"IN AN **EXCLUSIVE STORY** THAT WILL ALMOST CERTAINLY WIN ME ALL THE AWARDS, THE **MOON-X ROCKET** SEEMS TO HAVE TAKEN OFF **THREE DAYS EARLY!**"

—Tiffany Fluffit

HEIST HALL OF FAME

It's time to learn some big bad history. From grand heists to legendary chases—and everything in between— the *former* Bad Guys can always learn a lot from the good ol' days and know that the future is even brighter. (Oh stop, you're making me tear up!)

Want to take a look at some of the coolest items in our crew's history? One ticket to the Heist Hall of Fame coming right up.

This mega meteorite harnesses a special energy that can even control minds. Professor Marmalade plotted to steal it and frame us—and he almost got away with it, too!

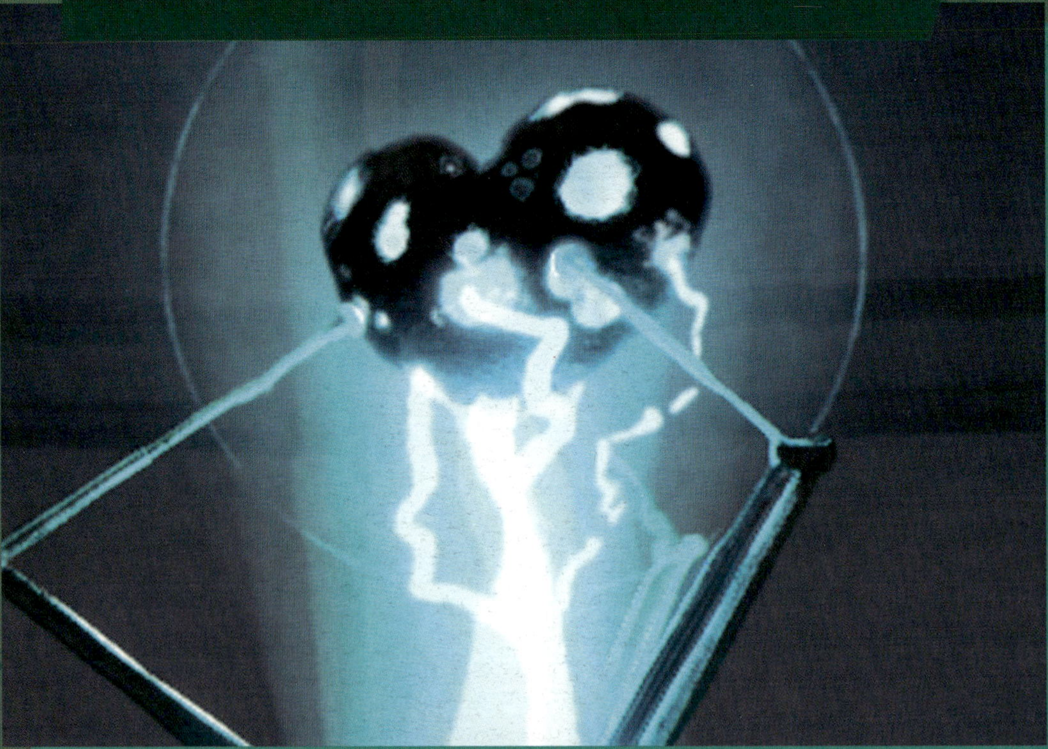

Now why would the little-Miss-perfect-power-suits governor have a Zumpango Diamond ring?

The Golden Dolphin is awarded to the *goodest* citizen! Way back when, the guys had an epic plan to wipe that smirk off the governor's fuzzy face and steal the award from right under her paws.

Here's the coolest car of all time! The Bad Guy mobile is a one-of-a-kind prototype—with *unlimited* horsepower! Stealing a getaway car to *use* as a getaway car? What a way to get off scot-free!

What does no job, no stolen loot, and no getaway car get you? A small, stalling, and seriously lame blue beater. This clunky compact car barely got me around Los Angeles. No one said it was easy to steer the crew in the right direction!

The Belt of Guatelamango is awarded to the mightiest *luchador* each year at the Lords of Lucha Tournament. This championship trophy is made of MacGuffinite—the very material Marmalade and the Bad Girls were seeking.

The MOON-X Rocket is the most sophisticated, luxurious, and expensive vehicle *ever* built. According to Mr. Moon himself, it's just like flying to the moon—in a yacht. Of course, it was the perfect target for Kitty Kat and crew to turn into a gold magnet.

Everything—from first-class security systems to the MOON-X launch site—is controlled by Mr. Moon himself with his custom-made fancy watch. Stealing the watch is the key to stealing the power!

EPIC AND NOT-SO-EPIC MOMENTS

Our crew has had some truly awesome adventures! But, sometimes it doesn't go so smoothly... Talk about courage, smarts, and maybe a little bit of recklessness.

Hey, who can blame us?

EPIC

NOT-SO-EPIC

BEST DRESSED

The key to every great heist is being able to move undetected. Thanks to Shark's supercool disguises, some of the most wanted guys in history are able to enter *anywhere*, *anytime*, without *anyone* noticing.

Way back when, we used these disguises to commit crime. But now, great disguises are even good for catching criminals and sneaking up on our enemies when they least expect it.

From awesome acting skills to crazy costumes, let's take a look at the crew's best disguises to date!

I'm Poodleton . . . Oliver Poodleton.

A drink for the pretty lady at the charity event? Be careful, she'll take a bite outta you!

Well, there goes our street cred! We don't look *so bad* anymore!

Hey there, son! How about playing catch with your old man?

You'll never see me coming! Time to fly to a billionaire's rooftop.

All clear on the roof! It's go time.

I'm in! All units are a go!

Weddings by ~~Marco~~ Big Tuna? *Jaw*-some!

That's called muscle, baby! Call me Clarence, the latest and greatest security guard.

I'm in position, ready to slither into any hard-to-reach places on this heist!

BREAKING NEWS

EXTRA! EXTRA!

READ ALL ABOUT . . . *US*!

You could say the guys are kind of a big deal. After all, the media has been covering our *where*abouts and *what*abouts for a looong time now. And hey, sometimes they do frame us for things that we don't do—but we gotta stay up-to-date on what the world thinks about us. Especially now that we've gone good and are *still* trying to prove it!

Not only do we love reading about *ourselves*, but the guys also always keep our fins, legs, paws, and tails on all future targets, enemies, and mysteries. We've gotta keep our pulse on this city! Capiche?

Want to know the best way to prepare for a heist? Research, research, research!

the_real_prf_marmalade Live Stream

Stream something good! This heart-melting video is sure to make the Bad Guys an overnight viral sensation!

BILLIONAIRE'S DIGEST MAGAZINE

FUN FACT:

YOU CAN LEARN A LOT ABOUT YOUR FOES FROM THE NEWS. CHECK IT OUT!

CRIMSON GOVERNOR! FOXINGTON'S SECRET LIFE REVEALED!

LIVE FROM CHANNEL 6 NEWS!

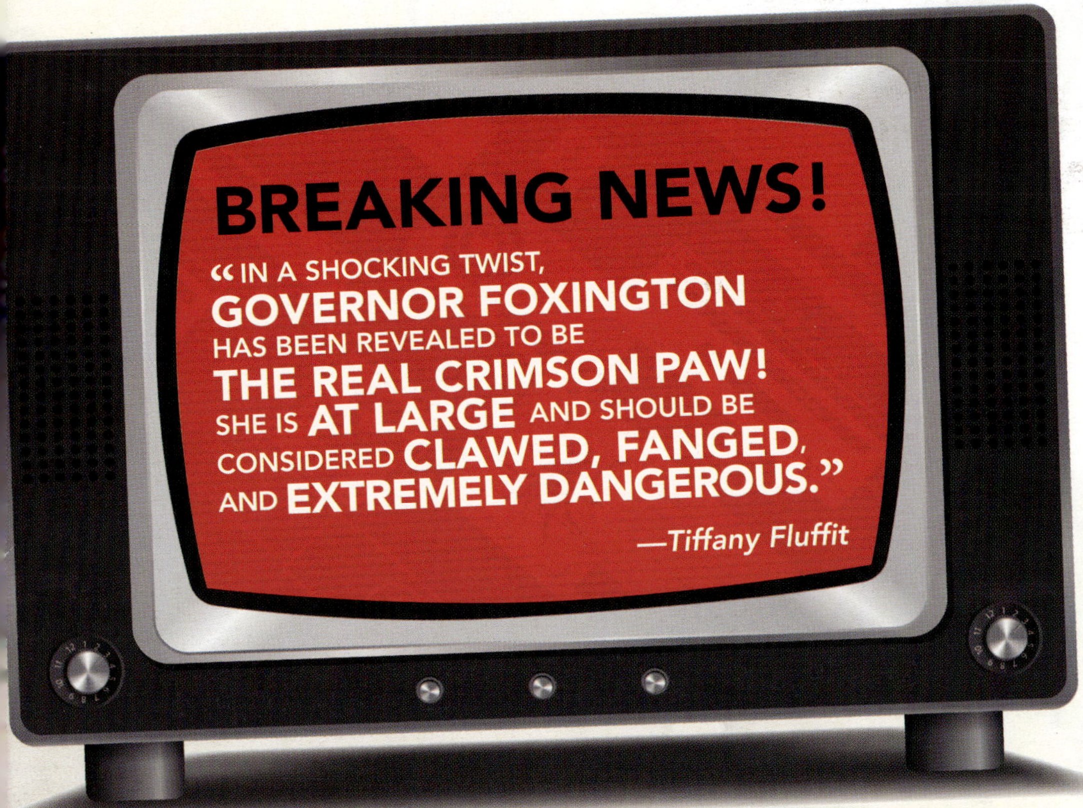

YOU'VE BEEN SELECTED!

You've outdone yourself, rookie. Congratulations! You've been recommended by Chief and identified as an ideal candidate for the brand-new International Super Galactic League of Protectors (ISGLOP)! Think you can handle a life of danger and excitement?

In order to know where we're going, we needed to revisit where we came from. From the baddest-of-the-bad missions to the save-the-world-style heists for good, the crew is always jumping into action and expecting the unexpected. Call me old-fashioned, but I love a good twist.

Going good wasn't a career move, after all. It was a true leap of faith! This way, I can *still* be myself, only this time, stop others from being bad in the process.

We're ready for another fresh start. If anyone understands that doing bad things in the past doesn't define you forever, we do! Now it's time to get to work busting bad guys. Are you in?

You're wagging now, pal. It feels so good to be good!

“THIS IS A CHANCE TO **WRITE YOUR OWN STORY.** TO FIND A BETTER LIFE FOR YOU AND YOUR FRIENDS. COME ON, **WHAT DO YOU HAVE TO LOSE?**”

—Governor Foxington